THIS BOOK BELONGS TO:

A BRIEF INSIGHT INTO ANCIENT GREEK HISTORY

ANCIENT GREEKS LIVED OVER 3000 YEARS AGO. THEIR CIVILISATIONS FOLLOWED A DARK AGE IN GREECE, WHICH IS THOUGHT TO HAVE ENDED IN 800 B.C. FOR THE MOST PART, ANCIENT GREECE WAS DIVIDED INTO SEVERAL SMALL CITY-STATES, EACH WITH THEIR OWN LAWS, CUSTOMS, AND RULERS. HOWEVER, IN THE 300S B.C., THESE SMALL CITY-STATES WERE FORCED TO UNITE UNDER ONE RULER: ALEXANDER THE GREAT. HE WAS THE FOUNDER OF THE ANCIENT GREEK EMPIRE, WHICH STRETCHED INTO EUROPE, EGYPT, AND SOUTH-WEST ASIA.

THE ANCIENT GREEKS WERE
DESCENDED FROM THE MYCENAEANS,
WHO WERE ALSO THE FIRST WRITERS
AND SPEAKERS OF 'ANCIENT GREEK'. A
FAMOUS LEGEND TELLS HOW, IN 1180
B.C., THE MIGHTY MYCENAEANS
CONQUERED THE CITY OF TROY – BY
HIDING INSIDE A GIANT WOODEN
HORSE! THE HORSE WAS LEFT OUTSIDE
THE CITY'S WALLS AND, THINKING IT A
GIFT, THE PEOPLE OF TROY WHEELED
IT INSIDE... ONLY FOR THE SNEAKY
MYCENAEAN SOLDIERS TO CREEP OUT
AND SEIZE THE CITY!

DID YOU KNOW THAT THE ANCIENT GREEKS INVENTED THE THEATRE? THEY LOVED WATCHING PLAYS, AND MOST CITIES HAD A THEATRE – SOME BIG ENOUGH TO HOLD 15,000 PEOPLE! ONLY MEN AND BOYS WERE ALLOWED TO BE ACTORS, AND THEY WORE MASKS, WHICH SHOWED THE AUDIENCE WHETHER THEIR CHARACTER WAS HAPPY OR SAD. SOME OF THE MASKS HAD TWO SIDES, SO THE ACTOR COULD TURN THEM AROUND TO CHANGE THE MOOD FOR EACH SCENE.

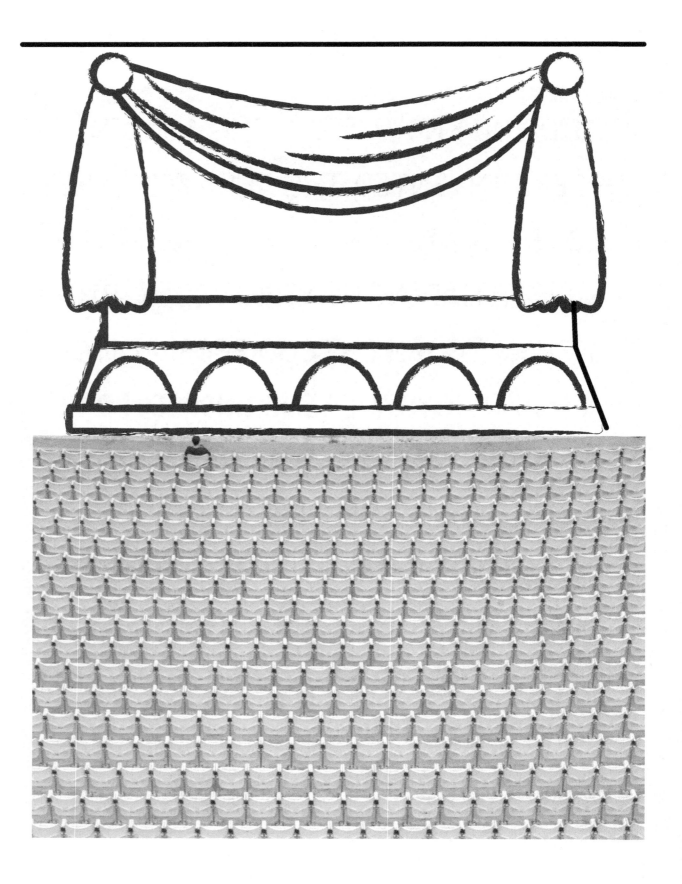

MOST ANCIENT GREEKS WORE **A CHITON**, WHICH WAS A LONG T-SHIRT MADE FROM ONE LARGE PIECE OF COTTON.
THE POOR SLAVES, HOWEVER, HAD TO MAKE DO WITH A LOINCLOTH (A SMALL STRIP OF CLOTH WRAPPED AROUND THE WAIST)!

THE ANCIENT GREEKS HELD MANY FESTIVALS IN HONOUR OF THEIR GODS. TO CELEBRATE THE GOD ZEUS, FOR EXAMPLE, THE FIRST GREEK OLYMPICS WERE HELD IN THE CITY OF OLYMPIA IN 776 B.C. AND ARE THOUGHT TO HAVE INSPIRED OUR OWN OLYMPIC GAMES!

THE WINNERS OF EACH EVENT WERE GIVEN A WREATH OF LEAVES, AND WHEN THEY RETURNED HOME, THEY WOULD BE GIVEN FREE MEALS AND THE BEST SEATS IN THE THEATRE!

ZEUS IS THE GOD OF THE SKY IN ANCIENT GREEK MYTHOLOGY. AS THE CHIEF GREEK DEITY, ZEUS IS CONSIDERED THE RULER, PROTECTOR, AND FATHER OF ALL GODS AND HUMANS. ZEUS IS OFTEN DEPICTED AS AN OLDER MAN WITH A BEARD AND IS REPRESENTED BY SYMBOLS SUCH AS THE LIGHTNING BOLT AND THE EAGLE.

THE ANCIENT GREEKS HELD MANY FESTIVALS IN HONOUR OF THEIR GODS. TO CELEBRATE THE GOD ZEUS, FOR EXAMPLE, THE FIRST GREEK OLYMPICS WERE HELD IN THE CITY OF OLYMPIA IN 776 B.C. AND ARE THOUGHT TO HAVE INSPIRED OUR OWN OLYMPIC GAMES!

THE WINNERS OF EACH EVENT WERE GIVEN A WREATH OF LEAVES, AND WHEN THEY RETURNED HOME, THEY WOULD BE GIVEN FREE MEALS AND THE BEST SEATS IN THE THEATRE!

STATUES OF GREEK GODS AND GODDESSES WERE PLACED INSIDE TEMPLES, THE MOST FAMOUS OF WHICH IS THE PARTHENON. THIS TEMPLE IN ATHENS WAS BUILT FOR THE GODDESS ATHENA, THE PROTECTOR OF THE CITY.

THE PARTHENON IS REGARDED AS AN ENDURING SYMBOL OF ANCIENT GREECE, DEMOCRACY AND WESTERN CIVILIZATION,[9] AND ONE OF THE WORLD'S GREATEST CULTURAL MONUMENTS.TO THE ATHENIANS WHO BUILT IT, THE PARTHENON, AND OTHER PERICLEAN MONUMENTS OF THE ACROPOLIS, WERE SEEN FUNDAMENTALLY AS A CELEBRATION OF HELLENIC VICTORY OVER THE PERSIAN INVADERS AND AS A THANKSGIVING TO THE GODS FOR THAT VICTORY.

THE PARTHENON ITSELF REPLACED AN OLDER TEMPLE OF ATHENA, WHICH HISTORIANS CALL THE PRE-PARTHENON OR OLDER PARTHENON, THAT WAS DEMOLISHED IN THE PERSIAN INVASION OF 480 BC. LIKE MOST GREEK TEMPLES, THE PARTHENON SERVED A PRACTICAL PURPOSE AS THE CITY TREASURY

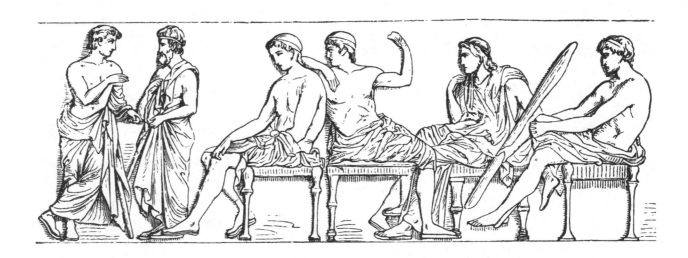

THE ANCIENT OLYMPIC GAMES WERE A SERIES OF ATHLETIC COMPETITIONS AMONG REPRESENTATIVES OF CITY-STATES AND ONE OF THE PANHELLENIC GAMES OF ANCIENT GREECE. THEY WERE HELD IN HONOR OF ZEUS, AND THE GREEKS GAVE THEM A MYTHOLOGICAL ORIGIN. THE FIRST OLYMPIC GAMES ARE TRADITIONALLY DATED TO 776 BC

EVENTS AT THE GREEK'S OLYMPICS INCLUDED WRESTLING, BOXING, LONG JUMP, JAVELIN, DISCUS AND CHARIOT RACING. BUT THOSE TAKING PART IN THE WRESTLING EVENT HAD TO BE THE TOUGHEST, AS THERE WERE HARDLY ANY RULES – AND THEY HAD TO COMPETE WITHOUT CLOTHES.

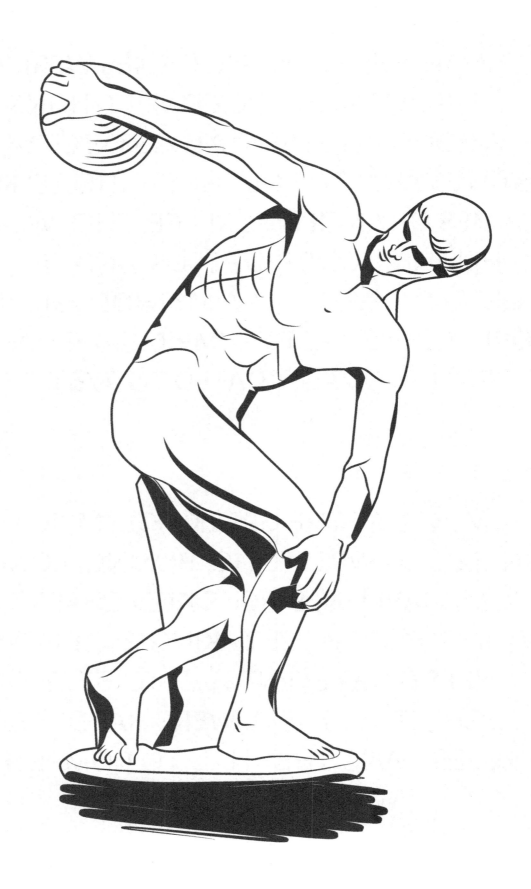

THE ANCIENT GREEKS HAD LOTS OF
STORIES TO HELP THEM LEARN ABOUT
THEIR WORLD.
THE GODS FEATURED HEAVILY IN THESE
TALES, AND SO DID MYTHOLOGICAL
MONSTERS - LIKE CERBERUS, A THREE-
HEADED DOG THAT GUARDED THE GATES
TO THE UNDERWORLD; MEDUSA, A
SLITHERY SORCERESS WHOSE LOOK
COULD TURN PEOPLE TO STONE; AND THE
CYCLOPS, WHO HAD ONE EYE IN THE
MIDDLE OF ITS FOREHEAD - YIKES! THESE
TALES ARE KNOWN AS GREEK
MYTHOLOGY

CERBERUS

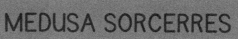

CYCLOP

IN GREEK TRADITION, A HIKETERIA WAS AN OLIVE BRANCH HELD BY SUPPLICANTS TO SHOW THEIR STATUS AS SUCH WHEN APPROACHING PERSONS OF POWER OR IN TEMPLES WHEN SUPPLICATING THE GODS.

IN GREEK MYTHOLOGY, ATHENA COMPETED WITH POSEIDON FOR POSSESSION OF ATHENS. POSEIDON CLAIMED POSSESSION BY THRUSTING HIS TRIDENT INTO THE ACROPOLIS, WHERE A WELL OF SEA-WATER GUSHED OUT. ATHENA TOOK POSSESSION BY PLANTING THE FIRST OLIVE TREE BESIDE THE WELL. THE COURT OF GODS AND GODDESSES RULED THAT ATHENA HAD THE BETTER RIGHT TO THE LAND BECAUSE SHE HAD GIVEN IT THE BETTER GIFT. OLIVE WREATHS WERE WORN BY BRIDES[4] AND AWARDED TO OLYMPIC VICTORS.

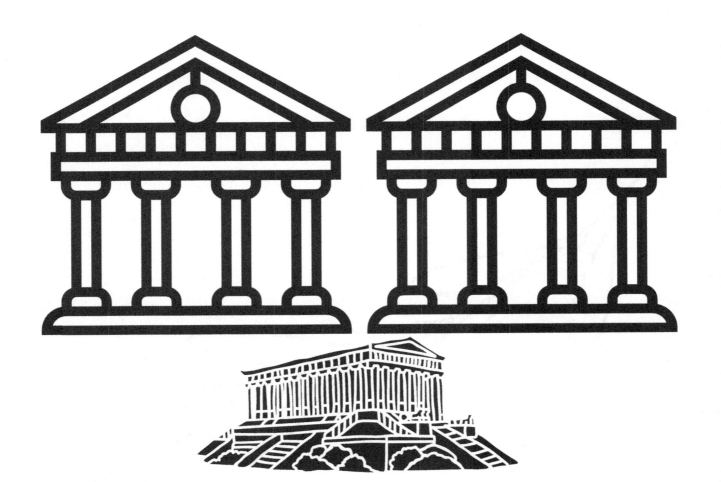

THE TEMPLE OF ARTEMIS OR ARTEMISION , ALSO KNOWN AS THE TEMPLE OF DIANA, WAS A GREEK TEMPLE DEDICATED TO AN ANCIENT, LOCAL FORM OF THE GODDESS ARTEMIS (ASSOCIATED WITH DIANA, A ROMAN GODDESS). IT WAS LOCATED IN EPHESUS (NEAR THE MODERN TOWN OF SELÇUK IN PRESENT-DAY TURKEY). IT WAS COMPLETELY REBUILT TWICE, ONCE AFTER A DEVASTATING FLOOD AND THREE HUNDRED YEARS LATER AFTER AN ACT OF ARSON, AND IN ITS FINAL FORM WAS ONE OF THE SEVEN WONDERS OF THE ANCIENT WORLD. BY 401 AD IT HAD BEEN RUINED OR DESTROYED. ONLY FOUNDATIONS AND FRAGMENTS OF THE LAST TEMPLE REMAIN AT THE SITE.

SOLON WAS ONE OF THE SEVEN WISE MEN OF GREECE AND DOMINATED ATHENIAN POLITICS FOR SEVERAL DECADES, BECOMING THE CITY'S CHIEF MAGISTRATE IN THE EARLY YEARS OF THE 6TH CENTURY BC (594-3 BC).

HE IS REMEMBERED PARTICULARLY FOR HIS EFFORTS TO LEGISLATE AGAINST POLITICAL, ECONOMIC AND MORAL DECLINE IN ARCHAIC ATHENS. HIS REFORMS FAILED IN THE SHORT TERM, YET HE IS OFTEN CREDITED WITH HAVING LAID THE FOUNDATIONS FOR ATHENIAN DEMOCRACY.

Solon

DRACHMA, SILVER COIN OF ANCIENT GREECE, DATING FROM ABOUT THE MID-6TH CENTURY BC, AND THE FORMER MONETARY UNIT OF MODERN GREECE.

THE DRACHMA WAS ONE OF THE WORLD'S EARLIEST COINS. ITS NAME DERIVES FROM THE GREEK VERB MEANING "TO GRASP," AND ITS ORIGINAL VALUE WAS EQUIVALENT TO THAT OF A HANDFUL OF ARROWS.

ALEXANDER III OF MACEDON (GREEK:ALÉXANDROS; 20/21 JULY 356 BC – 10/11 JUNE 323 BC), COMMONLY KNOWN AS ALEXANDER THE GREAT, WAS A KING OF THE ANCIENT GREEK KINGDOM OF MACEDON.[A] A MEMBER OF THE ARGEAD DYNASTY, HE WAS BORN IN PELLA–A CITY IN ANCIENT GREECE–IN 356 BC. HE SUCCEEDED HIS FATHER KING PHILIP II TO THE THRONE AT THE AGE OF 20, AND SPENT MOST OF HIS RULING YEARS CONDUCTING A LENGTHY MILITARY CAMPAIGN THROUGHOUT WESTERN ASIA AND NORTHEASTERN AFRICA. BY THE AGE OF THIRTY, HE HAD CREATED ONE OF THE LARGEST EMPIRES IN HISTORY, STRETCHING FROM GREECE TO NORTHWESTERN INDIA. HE WAS UNDEFEATED IN BATTLE AND IS WIDELY CONSIDERED TO BE ONE OF HISTORY'S GREATEST AND MOST SUCCESSFUL MILITARY COMMANDERS.

A BATTLE SCENE WITH ALEXANDER THE GREAT

THE INFLUENCE OF WINE IN ANCIENT GREECE HELPED ANCIENT GREECE TRADE WITH NEIGHBORING COUNTRIES AND REGIONS. MANY MANNERISMS AND CULTURAL ASPECTS WERE ASSOCIATED WITH WINE. IT LED TO GREAT CHANGE IN ANCIENT GREECE AS WELL.

THE PEOPLES OF THE MEDITERRANEAN BEGAN TO EMERGE FROM BARBARISM WHEN THEY LEARNED TO CULTIVATE THE OLIVE AND THE VINE.[I]HE GREEKS DILUTED THEIR WINE WITH WATER (I PART WINE TO 3 PARTS WATER).

PERICLES (495 - 429 BC) WAS A GREEK STATESMAN AND GENERAL OF ATHENS DURING ITS GOLDEN AGE. PERICLES WAS PROMINENT AND INFLUENTIAL IN ATHENIAN POLITICS, PARTICULARLY BETWEEN THE GRECO-PERSIAN WARS AND THE PELOPONNESIAN WAR, AND WAS ACCLAIMED BY THUCYDIDES, A CONTEMPORARY HISTORIAN, AS "THE FIRST CITIZEN OF ATHENS". HE TURNED THE DELIAN LEAGUE INTO AN ATHENIAN EMPIRE AND LED HIS COUNTRYMEN DURING THE FIRST TWO YEARS OF THE PELOPONNESIAN WAR. THE PERIOD DURING WHICH HE LED ATHENS, ROUGHLY FROM 461 TO 429 BC, IS SOMETIMES KNOWN AS THE "AGE OF PERICLES", BUT THE PERIOD THUS DENOTED CAN INCLUDE TIMES AS EARLY AS THE PERSIAN WARS OR AS LATE AS THE FOLLOWING CENTURY.

PERICLES PROMOTED THE ARTS AND LITERATURE, AND IT IS PRINCIPALLY THROUGH HIS EFFORTS THAT ATHENS ACQUIRED THE REPUTATION OF BEING THE EDUCATIONAL AND CULTURAL CENTER OF THE ANCIENT GREEK WORLD. HE STARTED AN AMBITIOUS PROJECT THAT GENERATED MOST OF THE SURVIVING STRUCTURES ON THE ACROPOLIS, INCLUDING THE PARTHENON.

PERICLES

PYTHAGORAS OF SAMOS[A] (C. 570 - C. 495 BC) WAS AN ANCIENT IONIAN GREEK PHILOSOPHER AND THE EPONYMOUS FOUNDER OF PYTHAGOREANISM. HIS POLITICAL AND RELIGIOUS TEACHINGS WERE WELL KNOWN IN MAGNA GRAECIA AND INFLUENCED THE PHILOSOPHIES OF PLATO, ARISTOTLE, AND, THROUGH THEM, WESTERN PHILOSOPHY. KNOWLEDGE OF HIS LIFE IS CLOUDED BY LEGEND, BUT HE APPEARS TO HAVE BEEN THE SON OF MNESARCHUS, A GEM-ENGRAVER ON THE ISLAND OF SAMOS. MODERN SCHOLARS DISAGREE REGARDING PYTHAGORAS'S EDUCATION AND INFLUENCES, BUT THEY DO AGREE THAT, AROUND 530 BC, HE TRAVELLED TO CROTON IN SOUTHERN ITALY, WHERE HE FOUNDED A SCHOOL IN WHICH INITIATES WERE SWORN TO SECRECY AND LIVED A COMMUNAL, ASCETIC LIFESTYLE. THIS LIFESTYLE ENTAILED A NUMBER OF DIETARY PROHIBITIONS, TRADITIONALLY SAID TO HAVE INCLUDED VEGETARIANISM, ALTHOUGH MODERN SCHOLARS DOUBT THAT HE EVER ADVOCATED FOR COMPLETE VEGETARIANISM.

PYTHAGORAS

PLATO (428/427 OR 424/423 - 348/347 BC) WAS AN ATHENIAN PHILOSOPHER DURING THE CLASSICAL PERIOD IN ANCIENT GREECE, FOUNDER OF THE PLATONIST SCHOOL OF THOUGHT AND THE ACADEMY, THE FIRST INSTITUTION OF HIGHER LEARNING IN THE WESTERN WORLD.HE IS WIDELY CONSIDERED ONE OF THE MOST IMPORTANT AND INFLUENTIAL INDIVIDUALS IN HUMAN HISTORY, AND THE PIVOTAL FIGURE IN THE HISTORY OF ANCIENT GREEK AND WESTERN PHILOSOPHY, ALONG WITH HIS TEACHER, SOCRATES, AND HIS MOST FAMOUS STUDENT, ARISTOTLE.PLATO HAS ALSO OFTEN BEEN CITED AS ONE OF THE FOUNDERS OF WESTERN RELIGION AND SPIRITUALITY.

PLATO

THE GORTYN LAW CODE GRANTS A MODICUM OF PROPERTY RIGHTS TO WOMEN IN THE CASE OF DIVORCE. DIVORCED WOMEN ARE ENTITLED TO ANY PROPERTY THAT THEY BROUGHT TO THE MARRIAGE AND HALF OF THE JOINT INCOME IF DERIVED FROM HER PROPERTY. THE CODE ALSO PROVIDES FOR A PORTION OF THE HOUSEHOLD PROPERTY.

UNLIKE SUCH GREEK CITY-STATES AS ATHENS, A CENTER FOR THE ARTS, LEARNING AND PHILOSOPHY, SPARTA WAS CENTERED ON A WARRIOR CULTURE. MALE SPARTAN CITIZENS WERE ALLOWED ONLY ONE OCCUPATION: SOLDIER. INDOCTRINATION INTO THIS LIFESTYLE BEGAN EARLY.

SPARTAN BOYS STARTED THEIR MILITARY TRAINING AT AGE 7, WHEN THEY LEFT HOME AND ENTERED THE AGOGE. THE BOYS LIVED COMMUNALLY UNDER AUSTERE CONDITIONS. THEY WERE SUBJECTED TO CONTINUAL PHYSICAL, COMPETITIONS (WHICH COULD INVOLVE VIOLENCE), GIVEN MEAGER RATIONS AND EXPECTED TO BECOME SKILLED AT STEALING FOOD, AMONG OTHER SURVIVAL SKILLS.

SPARTAN

SPEARS AND PIKES WERE THE PRIMARY WEAPONS OF THE SPARTAN MILITARY AND PROVIDED LONG-RANGE CAPABILITIES DURING BATTLES. BOTH WEAPONS WERE CONSTRUCTED USING WOOD FOR THE SHAFT AND IRON FOR THE POINTED ENDS.

THE SECONDARY WEAPON USED BY THE SPARTAN INFANTRY WAS A SHORT SWORD KNOWN AS A "XIPHOS." THIS WEAPON WAS MEANT TO COMPLEMENT THE LONGER SPEAR AND PROVIDE SOLDIERS WITH A WEAPON THEY COULD USE IN CLOSE COMBAT, WHERE THE RANGE OF THE SPEAR OR PIKE BECAME USELESS. THE SWORD WAS SHAPED LIKE A LONG LEAF AND WAS TYPICALLY 2-FEET LONG. IT WAS PRIMARILY USED IN A SLASHING AND SPEARING MOTION DURING BATTLE.

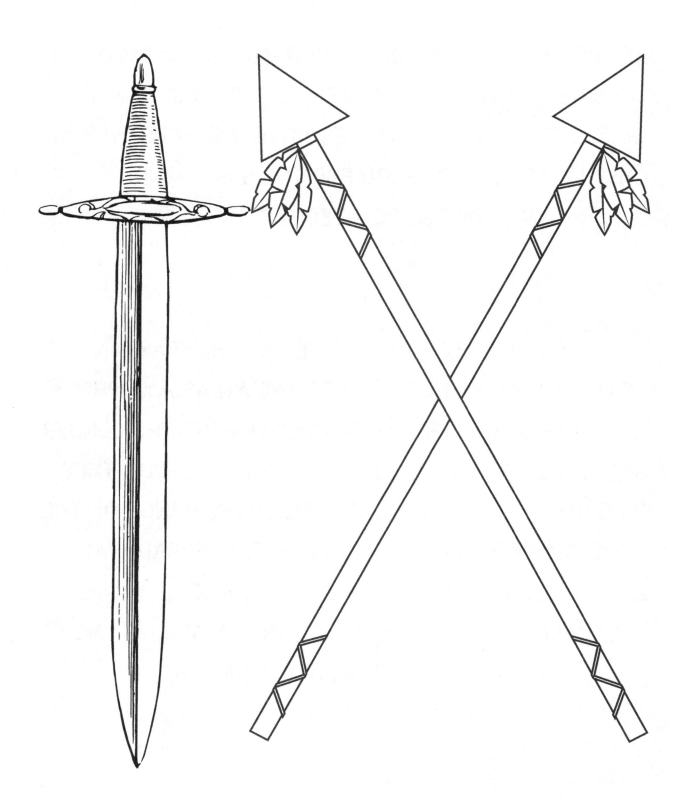

SHIELD
AND HELMET

ANCIENT GREEK ARCHITECTURE IS BEST KNOWN FROM ITS TEMPLES, MANY OF WHICH ARE FOUND THROUGHOUT THE REGION, AND THE PARTHENON IS A PRIME EXAMPLE OF THIS, MOSTLY AS RUINS BUT MANY SUBSTANTIALLY INTACT.

THE SECOND IMPORTANT TYPE OF BUILDING THAT SURVIVES ALL OVER THE HELLENIC WORLD IS THE OPEN-AIR THEATRE, WITH THE EARLIEST DATING FROM AROUND 525-480 BC. OTHER ARCHITECTURAL FORMS THAT ARE STILL IN EVIDENCE ARE THE PROCESSIONAL GATEWAY (PROPYLON), THE PUBLIC SQUARE (AGORA) SURROUNDED BY STORIED COLONNADE (STOA), THE TOWN COUNCIL BUILDING (BOULEUTERION), THE PUBLIC MONUMENT, THE MONUMENTAL TOMB (MAUSOLEUM) AND THE STADIUM.

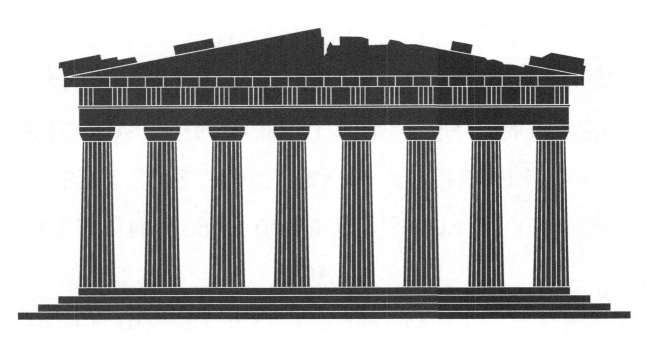

THE POTTERY OF ANCIENT GREECE FROM C. 1000 TO C. 400 BCE PROVIDES NOT ONLY SOME OF THE MOST DISTINCTIVE VASE SHAPES FROM ANTIQUITY BUT ALSO SOME OF THE OLDEST AND MOST DIVERSE REPRESENTATIONS OF THE CULTURAL BELIEFS AND PRACTICES OF THE ANCIENT GREEKS

THE CLAY (KERAMOS) TO PRODUCE POTTERY (KERAMEIKOS) WAS READILY AVAILABLE THROUGHOUT GREECE, ALTHOUGH THE FINEST WAS ATTIC CLAY, WITH ITS HIGH IRON CONTENT GIVING AN ORANGE-RED COLOUR WITH A SLIGHT SHEEN WHEN FIRED AND THE PALE BUFF OF CORINTH. CLAY WAS GENERALLY PREPARED AND REFINED IN SETTLING TANKS SO THAT DIFFERENT CONSISTENCIES OF MATERIAL COULD BE ACHIEVED DEPENDING ON THE VESSEL TYPES TO BE MADE WITH IT.

GREEKS USED TO BRING ANIMALS AS SACRIFICE,
IT WAS PART OF THEIR LERIGIOUS CUSTOMS.

THE BEST ANIMAL OR BEST SHARE OF THE ANIMAL IS
THE ONE PRESENTED FOR OFFERING.

HERA IS THE GODDESS OF WOMEN, MARRIAGE, FAMILY AND CHILDBIRTH IN ANCIENT GREEK RELIGION AND MYTHOLOGY, ONE OF THE TWELVE OLYMPIANS AND THE SISTER AND WIFE OF ZEUS. SHE IS THE DAUGHTER OF THE TITANS CRONUS AND RHEA. HERA RULES OVER MOUNT OLYMPUS AS QUEEN OF THE GODS. A MATRONLY FIGURE, HERA SERVED AS BOTH THE PATRONESS AND PROTECTRESS OF MARRIED WOMEN, PRESIDING OVER WEDDINGS AND BLESSING MARITAL UNIONS. ONE OF HERA'S DEFINING CHARACTERISTICS IS HER JEALOUS AND VENGEFUL NATURE AGAINST ZEUS' NUMEROUS LOVERS AND ILLEGITIMATE OFFSPRING, AS WELL AS THE MORTALS WHO CROSS HER.

ANOTHER INTERESTING FACT
ABOUT ANCIENT GREECE IS THAT
SLAVES WERE TRADED FOR SALT.
THAT GAVE THE RISE TO THE
COMMON EXPRESSION "NOT
WORTH HIS SALT".

ARISTARCHUS OF SAMOS WAS AN ANCIENT GREEK MATHEMATICIAN AND ASTRONOMER WHO FIRST PROPOSED THE THEORY THAT THE PLANETS ORBIT THE SUN. HE ALSO THEORISED THAT THE STARS ARE UNMOVING DISTANT SUNS. FURTHER STATING THAT THE SIZE OF THE UNIVERSE IS MUCH BIGGER THAN HIS CONTEMPORARIES BELIEVED.

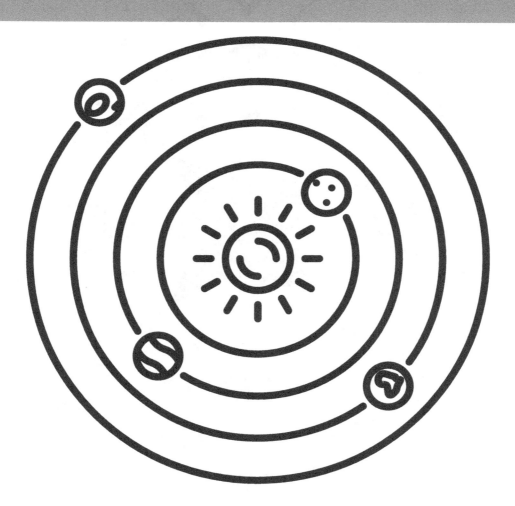

Color this mandala with traditional Greek traditional elements

This temple is ruined, can you rebuild it?

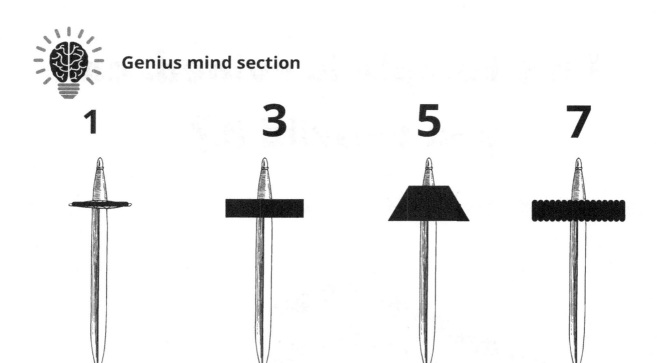

FOUR SWORDS ARE WAITING FOR THEIR MASTER TO START THE TRAININGS. TRY TO FIND THE OWNER OF THE SWORD.

* Nicos owns one of the highest numbered sword.

* The number of Kostas's sward is greater than the number of Nicos's and Michalis's sword

* David owns a numbered higher than Michalis's sword.

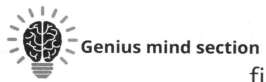

Help the man to
find his way toward the temple

THE GREEKS OFTEN ATE DINNER WHILE LYING ON THEIR SIDES. THEY INVENTED THE YO-YO WHICH IS CONSIDERED THE 2ND OLDEST TOY IN THE WORLD AFTER THE DOLL. ABOUT ONE THIRD OF THE POPULATION OF SOME CITY-STATES WERE SLAVES.ANCIENT GREEKS WERE HOSPITABLE EVEN WHEN THEY DID NOT WANT TO BE. THEY OFFERED FOOD, SHELTER AND PROTECTION TO TRAVELERS WITHOUT QUESTION. WHILE IT IS UNCLEAR WHETHER ANCIENT GREEKS WERE HOSPITABLE DUE TO THEIR FEAR OF THE GODS OR WHETHER THEY WERE SIMPLY DOING THEIR BROTHERLY DUTY, IT IS CLEAR THAT HOSPITALITY WAS AN IMPORTANT ASPECT OF LIFE.LOYALTY IS PERHAPS THE MOST INFLUENTIAL VALUE OF ANCIENT GREEK CIVILIZATION. LOYALTY WAS EMBEDDED IN EVERYTHING THE GREEKS DID. THEY BELIEVED IN LOYALTY TO THE FAMILY, THE COMMUNITY AND MOST IMPORTANTLY TO THE GODS. LOYALTY TO THE FAMILY MEANT DOING WHAT WAS BEST FOR YOUR FAMILY.

1 .WHICH TOY WAS INVENTED FIRST IN THE WORLD?

2 IN YOUR OPINION, WHY IS GREECE CONSIDERED THE FOUNDATION OF WESTERN CIVILIZATION?

3 WHY DO YOU THINK THE GREEKS WERE LOYAL TO GODS, FAMILY AND STATE?

THANK YOU

WE HOPE YOU ENJOYED OUR
BOOK.
AS A SMALL FAMILY
COMPANY YOUR
FEEDBACK IS
VERY IMPORTANT
FOR US.
PLEASE LET US KNOW HOW
YOU LIKED
OUR BOOK AT:

NATYROSSY@GMAIL.COM